HOW DID IT HAI
THE
VIETNAM WAR

Clive Gifford

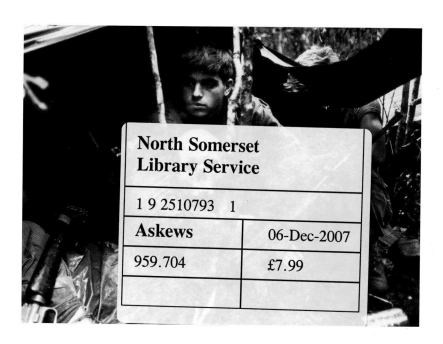

First published in 2005 by Franklin Watts
Reprinted 2007

Copyright © 2005 Arcturus Publishing Limited

Franklin Watts
338 Euston Road, London, NW1 3BH

Franklin Watts Australia
Level 17/207 Kent Street, Sydney, NSW 2000

Produced by Arcturus Publishing Limited
26/27 Bickels Yard, 151–153 Bermondsey Street
London SE1 3HA

Series concept: Alex Woolf
Editor: Philip de Ste. Croix
Designer: Stonecastle Graphics
Picture researcher: Thomas Mitchell

Picture credits:
All the photographs in this book were supplied by
Getty Images and are reproduced here with their
permission. The photographs appearing on the pages
listed below are Time Life images.
Time Life Pictures/Getty Images: 9, 18, 20, 21, 22,
27, 30, 33, 34, 42, 45.

A CIP catalogue record for this book is available
from the British Library

Dewey Decimal Classification Number: 959.704'3

ISBN: 978-0-7496-7725-1

Printed in China

Franklin Watts is a division of
Hachette Children's Books

Contents

1 Two Vietnams 4

2 Increasing US Involvement 10

3 The Height of Battle 20

4 Mounting Opposition 30

5 The Long Road to Peace 36

Vietnam Timeline 46

Glossary 47

Further Information 47

Index 48

1 Two Vietnams

The Vietnam War was a conflict that lasted from the 1950s until 1975. It was a struggle by South Vietnam, the United States and its allies to prevent the communists of North Vietnam from uniting North and South Vietnam under a communist government. Although primarily a military conflict, the burden of the war fell heavily on civilians in both North and South Vietnam. Over two million civilians and military personnel lost their lives during the war.

Vietnam is located in south-east Asia. It is bordered by China to the north, and to the east and south the South China Sea separates it from Indonesia and the Philippines. Together with Cambodia and Laos, its neighbours to the west, it was known in the nineteenth and early twentieth centuries as French Indo-China. France took control of Vietnam over a thirty-year period beginning in the late 1850s.

Colonial Powers

France was far from the only colonial power operating in the region. The Dutch and British controlled what is modern day Indonesia, the British held colonies in Burma (now Myanmar) and Malaya and, in 1898, the United States defeated the Spanish to establish a military presence in the Philippines. The colonial powers were drawn to the region for its shipping links and the land's resources that included spices, metals, sugar, rubber, coal and rice. These resources were exploited and transported out of Vietnam under French rule without the local people benefiting from them. Although a handful of Vietnamese became wealthy working with the French, the vast majority suffered. Food became scarce for ordinary people while taxes were high. Some Vietnamese pleaded with their local governments for help but these authorities had been stripped of influence and finances and had no real power to make a difference.

Opposition to French rule grew in many areas of Vietnam. Many small uprisings were ruthlessly dealt with by the French authorities during the 1920s and 1930s. Some rebels preferred to organize in secret, and these movements gradually grew in strength. Amongst them were a group of communists who were set on Vietnamese independence. They were led by Ho Chi Minh and Vo Nguyen Giap. In 1941 they formed the Vietnam Doc Lap Dong Minh Hoi – the League for the Independence of Vietnam – better known as the Vietminh.

This photograph shows Ho Chi Minh c.1940, around the time he was forming what would become the Vietminh to fight Japanese and French occupation of his home country. Ho defiantly told the French in the late 1940s that 'You can kill ten of my men for every one I kill of yours. But even at those odds, you will lose and I will win.'

By the time the Vietminh was formed, the Second World War (1939–45) was underway. France was quickly defeated by Germany and was not capable of defending its colonies in Asia. Japan invaded French Indo-China and by July 1941 had forced the French to let them run the colony. The Japanese stripped Vietnam of resources, leaving hundreds of thousands of Vietnamese to die of starvation. Opposition to Japanese rule was harshly dealt with but, by 1944, the Vietminh was strong enough to begin resistance attacks on Japanese outposts in northern Vietnam. By the beginning of 1945, the Vietminh forces, commanded by Giap, had risen to over 5,000, and controlled parts of northern Vietnam.

Japanese forces move further into French Indo-China during the Second World War. Japan stationed an estimated 30,000 troops in Indo-China and used its airstrips as military airbases. During the occupation, a famine broke out in the Tonkin region, a major source of rice production. Japanese forces did not move stored rice and foods to this region and around a quarter of the population died as a result.

VOICES FROM THE PAST

Ho Chi Minh

The son of a peasant teacher, Ho Chi Minh left Vietnam in 1911 as a kitchen hand on a French passenger liner and travelled extensively in Europe and Asia as well as visiting the United States. A passionate advocate of Vietnamese independence, he became a communist in 1920 and a founder member of the French Communist Party. His twin aims were to build an independent Vietnam free of foreign control and a nation ruled as a communist society. In his declaration of independence for Vietnam in 1945 he stated:

'*For more than eighty years, the French imperialists, abusing the standard of Liberty, Equality, and Fraternity, have violated our Fatherland and oppressed our fellow-citizens...The entire Vietnamese people are determined to sacrifice their lives and property, in order to safeguard their independence and freedom.*'

Ho Chi Minh, *Selected Works Volume 3* (Hanoi, 1960–1962)

The Return of French Occupation

Following the dropping of atomic bombs on the cities of Hiroshima and Nagasaki, Japan surrendered in August 1945. Japanese forces were ordered to leave Vietnam, and the French believed that it would be easy to regain control of its colonies in the region. However, the Vietminh acted quickly. In September 1945, they swept through the country's two largest cities, Hanoi in the north and Saigon in the south. In the north, they deposed the emperor, Bao Dai, and Ho Chi Minh declared an independent Vietnam. Ho appealed to foreign powers to recognize his country's independence from French rule but within three months 50,000 French troops were back in the region.

Four years later, Bao Dai was brought back from exile in Hong Kong by the French and installed as a leader under their control.

From 1946 to 1954, a period known as the First Indochina War, French and Vietminh forces engaged in sporadic fighting. The Vietminh built up their strength in isolated, northern parts of the country from which they carried out attacks on French targets. The Vietminh received a critical boost to their fortunes when China became a communist country under the leadership of Mao Zedong in 1949. The communist government of China was sympathetic to the communists in Vietnam and supplied them with modern weapons and other equipment. These supplies enabled the Vietminh to step up the frequency and ferocity of their attacks. Even so, on several occasions when the Vietminh attempted a massed battle, they were badly defeated by superior French weapons. In a January 1951 battle 50 km north of Hanoi, for example, Vietminh casualties numbered 14,000 injured or killed out of a total force of 20,000.

Vo Nguyen Giap, however, proved an excellent military leader. He learned from his mistakes, and developed hit-and-run style guerrilla warfare techniques to attack French forces. Knowledge of local terrain allowed a force to mount a rapid attack, then disappear back into dense tropical jungle where the men could hide and live off the land for long periods. At the same time, the Vietminh forces were under instruction to influence ordinary civilians whenever possible. Vietminh soldiers were ordered to be polite and fair, to return anything borrowed and not to steal or bully. Support for the Vietminh grew as a result, especially in northern Vietnam, and recruits swelled the ranks of their forces.

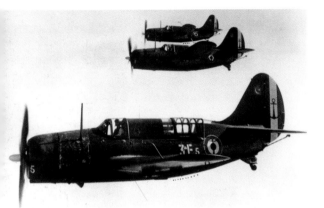

Three French airforce fighter bombers head to Dien Bien Phu to support their ground forces' battle against the Vietminh. The French lost forty-eight aircraft and two helicopters to enemy fire, and a further 167 were damaged during the two-month-long conflict.

Under Pressure

By 1953, the French forces in Vietnam, commanded by General Henri Navarre, were under severe pressure to win a major victory over the increasingly popular Vietminh. Navarre chose the site of Dien Bien Phu for a large-scale pitched battle with the Vietminh. However, his tactics proved disastrous, and the Vietminh lay siege and triumphed. During the siege, the French appealed to the United States for major military assistance but the US wanted other allies to commit to military action as well as themselves. Before the battle at Dien Bien Phu, a peace conference had been announced for the spring of 1954. Britain's foreign secretary, Anthony Eden, favoured a negotiated settlement rather than military action. Other nations were also reluctant to engage in military action, especially as the peace conference was already scheduled.

The conference was held in the Swiss city of Geneva and attended by representatives from France, Britain, the United States, China, the Soviet Union and the three French Indo-China nations: Vietnam, Cambodia and Laos. The conference resulted in the publication of a

Troops from the French Expeditionary Forces man their trenches during the siege of Dien Bien Phu. The battle was the fiercest the French endured during their occupation of Vietnam. Over 3,400 captured French prisoners were not returned for some four months after the end of the conflict.

TURNING POINT !

The siege of Dien Bien Phu !

In November 1953, the French constructed a large defensive complex at Dien Bien Phu, close to the border with Laos. It was designed to block Vietminh forces from using one of their key supply routes from Laos into South Vietnam and to lure the Vietminh into a large-scale battle. This sort of battle was the type the French were most confident of winning. However, Dien Bien Phu was situated in a valley and the Vietminh forces occupied positions in the hills to surround the French, digging giant tunnels to get closer and closer. They also hauled Chinese-made anti-aircraft guns and heavy artillery up mountainsides to bombard the French below. For 55 days, beginning on 11 March 1954, over 40,000 Vietminh troops lay siege to Dien Bien Phu. Its airstrip was shelled heavily to prevent reinforcements and supplies from reaching the French by air. By early May, the French forces had suffered an estimated 7,000 casualties. On 7 May the French surrendered and the next day the French government announced its intention of withdrawing from Vietnam.

The division of Vietnam created two states: the Democratic Republic of Vietnam in the North and the Republic of Vietnam in the South. Between them was a demilitarized zone (DMZ) some 10 km wide that was not occupied by either side's military forces. It was designed to act as a buffer between the two countries until the reunification elections in 1956.

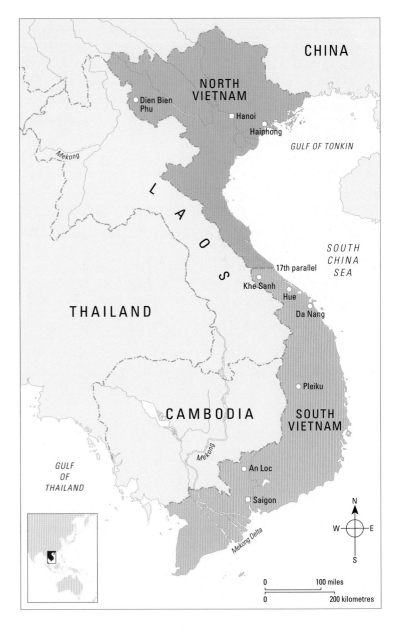

series of documents known as the Geneva Accords. Independence for Cambodia and Laos was granted with free elections to be held in 1955. The issue of Vietnam proved more complex. The country was to be temporarily divided by a horizontal line running through the line of geographical latitude known as 17th parallel. The Vietminh would withdraw to the northern portion – North Vietnam – under a communist government led by Ho Chi Minh, while the French would withdraw to South Vietnam. An election for reunifying the two halves was to be held in 1956.

HOW DID IT HAPPEN?

Could Vietnam have stayed as one nation in the 1950s?

Some historians believe that a concerted effort by the major powers at the Geneva Conference could have kept Vietnam united as a single country and that its division into two made further conflict inevitable. Others believe that granting Vietnam independence as a single country ruled by either a communist regime sympathetic to China and the Soviet Union or a non-communist government allied to the United States would have escalated the already increasing tension between the superpowers. Andrew Wiest states that 'In the end the superpowers did not want to risk global war over Vietnam' and dividing the country was the only way, at the time, that leaders felt this could be avoided.

Andrew Wiest, *The Vietnam War: 1956–1975* (Osprey, 2002)

The various delegations and their advisors take the table at the Geneva Conferences held from 26 April to 21 July 1954 and attended by France, the UK, the United States, China, the Soviet Union, Cambodia, Laos and Vietnam. A Vietminh delegation represented the interests of the communist Vietnamese. At the end of the conference, an uneasy compromise was reached with the temporary division of Vietnam into two halves.

2 Increasing US Involvement

An atomic bomb test in 1950 sends a tell-tale mushroom-shaped cloud into the atmosphere high above the Pacific Ocean island test site.

By the time that Vietnam was divided in two following the Geneva Conference of 1954, the Soviet Union and the United States had already emerged as the world's two leading nations. Having been allies in the conflict against Germany and Japan during the Second World War, the two countries found themselves at odds over many issues facing the world after the war and were deeply fearful and suspicious of each other's intentions and of their differing political systems.

Both superpowers worked feverishly to improve their own national security. Weapons were designed, built and stockpiled in increasingly large numbers and by the mid-1950s, with the advent of nuclear weapons, both superpowers were aware of the massive damage and destruction that their respective weapons could do. Both sides sought to avoid a direct confrontation but continued to build their influence around the globe.

The Policy of Containment

The superpowers formed military alliances with other countries, donating aid, equipment and weapons to assist the governments of nations that were sympathetic to them. They also sought, in some countries, to topple leaderships that were antagonistic towards their views, so that they could be replaced with friendlier regimes. For example, the Soviets invaded Hungary in 1956 while the US trained and supported rebels who invaded and toppled the government of Guatemala in 1954.

Leading politicians and military figures in the United States were deeply hostile towards the Soviet Union and its communist political system, which they feared would threaten their American way of life.

VOICES FROM THE PAST

The domino theory

To justify support for South Vietnam, US president Dwight D. Eisenhower and his advisors put forward the 'domino theory'. They argued that if South Vietnam fell to communism, other nations in the region, such as Laos, Thailand and Indonesia, would quickly follow. Eisenhower explained:

'You have a row of dominoes set up, you knock over the first one, and what will happen to the last one is the certainty that it will go over very quickly. So you could have a beginning of a disintegration that would have the most profound influences... Asia, after all, has already lost some 450 million of its peoples to the Communist dictatorship, and we simply can't afford greater losses.'

President Dwight D. Eisenhower – President Press Conference, 7 April 1954. Quoted in Stanley Karnow, *Vietnam: A History* (Penguin, 1991)

Russian tanks surround the parliament building in Budapest on 12 November 1956. The Soviet Union invaded Hungary to suppress a popular uprising in support of Imre Nagy's government, which was seeking greater independence from Soviet control. The willingness of the Soviet communist government to impose its will in eastern Europe by force alarmed politicians in the United States, and contributed to the climate of fear about the spread of communism that gripped the country during the 1950s.

They feared communism's spread to other countries and adopted a policy of containment. This was an attempt to halt the spread of communism to non-communist nations without provoking direct military action against the Soviet Union in the hope that the Soviet Union's communist regime would eventually collapse.

The US policy of containment was applied during the Korean War (1950–53). Korea was divided into two halves, North and South, in the aftermath of the Second World War. In 1950, the communist North, under leader Kim Il-Sung, mounted an invasion of South Korea in an attempt to reunify the country. The United Nations sent troops to South Korea from a number of countries, but the force was dominated by Americans. China, a

US troops march along a road towards the Korean city of Seoul after the September 1950 troop landings on the west coast of Korea at Inchon, some 35 km from Seoul. Under the command of General Douglas MacArthur, the daring action surprised the North Korean forces. The landings were one of the few major US successes of the Korean War.

neighbour of Korea, supported and armed communist North Korea. The resulting war was bloody with over three million deaths including some 37,000 Americans. In 1953, Korea was divided and remains so to the present day.

VOICES FROM THE PAST

Korean War critics

The Korean War was a brutal conflict and a number of people in the United States criticized the way American forces had been deployed. Running against Eisenhower in the 1952 presidential election, Adlai Stevenson asserted:

'We are fighting in Korea, [Eisenhower] declares, because the American Government grossly underestimated the Soviet threat; because the Government allowed America to become weak; because American weakness compelled us to withdraw our forces from Korea; because we abandoned China to the communists; and, finally, because we announced to all the world that we had written off most of the Far East.'

Adlai Stevenson, speech, Louisville (27 September 1952)

Vietnam Divided

The following year at the 1954 Geneva Conference, Vietnam was divided temporarily. Few parties left Geneva entirely satisfied with the result. Ho Chi Minh and the Vietminh were frustrated that they had been unable to take over more of Vietnam and that the elections were to be postponed until 1956. Ho's popularity made him a strong favourite to win a national election if it was held immediately. By contrast, the South Vietnamese were unhappy with the division of their country and the loss of so much territory. They were deeply fearful of a North Vietnam run by the communist Vietminh. The United States saw losing North Vietnam to communism as a major setback. It now feared for the future of South Vietnam and was determined to prevent another part of Asia from falling to communism.

The United States had given aid to France during France's conflict with the Vietminh. The US now decided to support an anti-communist government in South Vietnam and to strengthen it so that it could become stable and capable of defending itself. Around the time of the Geneva Conference, Ngo Dinh Diem was made Vietnamese Prime

Ho Chi Minh attends a youth rally in North Vietnam in 1955. During the same year, his government began major land reforms in North Vietnam, redistributing land from landlords and wealthier North Vietnamese to the poor and the landless. This resulted in the imprisonment and execution of many North Vietnamese.

Minister by Bao Dai. Diem, fearful of the communists in the north, had refused to accept the decisions of the Geneva conferences and sought American support for his position. Diem did not impress some members of the US government but nevertheless the US supported his leadership in South Vietnam. It did so partly because he was fervently anti-communist, partly because he was already in a position of power and partly, in the words of US Secretary of State John Foster Dulles, 'We have accepted him because we knew of no one better.'

Growing Unrest

In October 1955, Ngo Dinh Diem replaced Bao Dai as head of state of South Vietnam after elections were held. The election was blatantly corrupt with Diem claiming to have won 98.2 percent of the vote. With Diem as leader, South Vietnam experienced troubled times. Upon the division of Vietnam, approximately 900,000 Vietnamese in the northern region, who did not want to be subject to communist rule, had moved to the south. Finding homes, land and work for these people should have been a priority for the new government. In addition, US president Dwight D. Eisenhower hoped that Diem would carry out reforms to help the peasants of South Vietnam obtain land on which to farm and live a more prosperous life. But Diem appeared to be interested in little more than securing his own position as leader. He did not make major land reforms and instead moved his own supporters into positions of power in local areas. These officials often helped force ordinary people to work for landowners and to pay cripplingly high taxes.

Against the advice of the United States, the South Vietnamese leader, Ngo Dinh Diem, announced the results of the 1954 election by claiming he had won 98.2 percent of the popular vote. The obviously rigged voting results upset many South Vietnamese.

Others suffered under Diem's regime as well. Sympathizers and followers of the Vietminh were hunted down and either executed or sent to re-education prison camps. The Buddhist majority in the country were also angered by what they saw as Diem's religious

A peasant farmer and his children collect at the gates of Cu Chi strategic hamlet in South Vietnam. After decades of oppression by their French rulers, many peasants had expected life to be better under Vietnamese rule. Yet under Ngo Dinh Diem, the fortunes of most ordinary South Vietnamese peasants did not improve. Increasing resentment at Diem's regime was stoked by communist sympathizers out in the countryside.

prejudice. Diem was a Catholic in a land where most people were Buddhist and he tended to appoint only other Catholics to important positions in his government.

Additional criticism of Diem's regime came from the north. Ho launched verbal attacks on Diem's leadership, which increased when it became clear in 1956 that Diem had no intention of allowing the free election to reunite the whole of Vietnam to take place. Ho's speeches were just one part of North Vietnam's response. The North Vietnamese built up the strength of its own regular army, the NVA, and forged stronger alliances with China and the Soviet Union. In secret, North Vietnam also encouraged the movement of communists, dubbed Viet Cong by the United States, from North Vietnam into South Vietnam.

Communist Infiltration

In 1959, the North Vietnamese began guerrilla warfare attacks, primarily against members of Diem's government. Between 1959 and 1961, an average of 4,000 officials were killed by Viet Cong forces each year. Also in 1959, the North Vietnamese started building the Ho Chi Minh Trail. This 20,000 km route was an elaborate system of mountain and jungle trails running south from North Vietnam along the South Vietnamese border with Laos and Cambodia. Almost the entire length of the trail lay just within the borders of these neutral countries, in the belief that the United States and South Vietnam forces would not invade neutral countries to attack the trail. Supplies were sent to South Vietnamese communists along this route as the Viet Cong's guerrilla warfare mounted.

In December 1960, the communists set up a political organization called the National Liberation Front (NLF). Its aims were to overthrow Diem and reunite North and South Vietnam. It quickly infiltrated many villages and towns and gained popularity in parts of South Vietnam. In 1962, Diem responded by moving peasants away from areas of the country where the NLF were strong into new, fortified villages. All over South Vietnam people were forced to leave their own villages and communities and to move away from sacred family burial grounds. This tactic, known as the Strategic Hamlets policy, caused more suffering for peasants and did little to stem the growing support for the NLF.

Female South Vietnamese guards are put through their drills at a strategic hamlet in 1962. The Strategic Hamlets policy upset many South Vietnamese who were moved away from the burial sites of their ancestors, had further to travel to work their fields, and who were required to construct the bamboo stockades surrounding their relocated village themselves.

More US Aid

By the time the Strategic Hamlets policy was underway, over 12,000 US military advisers were present in South Vietnam. Two years earlier, the number had been just 700. John F. Kennedy had become US president at the start of 1961 and had promised during his election campaign to be tough on communism. He stepped up the levels of aid granted to South Vietnam and, in December 1961, announced increased numbers of US advisers and assistants to the country. Kennedy was reluctant to send combat troops openly to Vietnam, however. Instead he continued to help build up the South Vietnamese army, the ARVN, so that South Vietnam could fight for itself.

The United States had spent hundreds of millions of dollars on equipping and training the ARVN since Diem's election in 1955. Yet,

VOICES FROM THE PAST

de Gaulle's warning to Kennedy

Kennedy was reluctant to send US combat troops into Vietnam and other leaders agreed. On a visit to France in 1961, Kennedy met with French president Charles de Gaulle, who warned:

'The more you become involved out there against communism, the more the communists will appear as the champions of national independence. ...You will sink step by step into a bottomless military and political quagmire, however much you spend in men and money.'

Quoted in Hugh Brogan, *Kennedy* (Longman, 1996)

the ARVN, which had grown in number to 170,000 men by 1963, was not an impressive force. Its soldiers had low morale and their commanders often argued. Viet Cong forces frequently outwitted them in surprise attacks or outfought them in pitched battles. In January 1963, for example, some 350 Viet Cong guerrillas were

Senator John F. Kennedy is showered in ticker tape as he campaigns for the US presidency in 1960. In his inaugural address as president, Kennedy stated 'Let every nation know, whether it wishes us well or ill, that we shall pay any price, bear any burden, meet any hardship, support any friend, oppose any foe, in order to assure the survival and the success of liberty.'

TURNING POINT
The Gulf Of Tonkin incident

Before the Gulf of Tonkin incident, US military involvement in Vietnam had been largely restricted to financial aid and advice, not major attacks on North Vietnam or a large scale deployment of US troops. That changed in the aftermath of one of a series of secret missions by US boats close to the North Vietnamese coastline. On 2 August 1964, the American destroyer, USS *Maddox*, was fired upon by North Vietnamese torpedo boats while in the Gulf of Tonkin. Johnson warned North Vietnam that any further aggressive action would lead to 'grave consequences'. Two days later, it appeared that the *Maddox* was again attacked, although this later turned out to be false. The US Congress, which believed the second attack had taken place, passed the Gulf of Tonkin Resolution on 7 August. The resolution allowed the President to take 'all necessary measures to repel attacks…and prevent further aggression'. It also stated that the president should assist any friendly south-east Asian state by taking 'all necessary steps, including the use of armed force…in defense of its freedom'. Johnson immediately retaliated with air strikes over North Vietnam.

An ARVN paratrooper threatens a captured member of the Viet Cong with a knife. Many ARVN soldiers fought with distinction throughout the Vietnam War, but the effectiveness of South Vietnam's army was often blighted by poor and corrupt leadership and low morale.

forced into a battle near the village of Ap Bac against over 2,000 ARVN soldiers backed by US helicopters. Despite the overwhelming odds, the Viet Cong triumphed, shooting down five helicopters while apparently losing only a handful of their own number. In an interview in September 1963, Kennedy admitted to frustration with the South Vietnamese forces: 'We can help them, we can give them equipment, we can send our men…as advisors, but they have to win it – the people of Vietnam – against the Communists.'

Diem Overthrown

Many South Vietnamese were more concerned with protesting against their own government than with fighting communism. The growing unrest in South Vietnam intensified when protests by Buddhists in 1963 led to thousands of Buddhist monks being arrested. Many were never seen again. The unrest extended to the army and on 1 November 1963, a military coup overthrew and killed Diem. The US government had known about the coup in advance but kept silent in the hope that it would lead to a stronger South Vietnamese government. If anything, the reverse was the case, as a series of unstable leaders and governments followed Diem. Later the same month, Kennedy was assassinated in Dallas, Texas, and Lyndon Johnson was sworn in as his successor.

Johnson and his advisers, including Secretary of Defense Robert McNamara, were confronted by a stark situation in 1964. South Vietnam needed far more military support from the USA to prevent the country from falling into communist hands. As plans and discussions were under way, an incident in the Gulf of Tonkin led to a resolution from the US Congress that effectively gave Johnson the power to massively increase US military involvement in Vietnam.

On 11 June 1963, Thich Quang Duc, a 67-year-old Buddhist monk, adopted the crossed-leg lotus position at a busy intersection in Saigon, the capital of South Vietnam. Covered in gasoline by colleagues, he lit a match and remained still as he burned to death in minutes in protest at the continued persecution of Buddhists in South Vietnam. The image shocked the entire world.

HOW DID IT HAPPEN?

Waiting for a trigger?

Was the US government committed to increasing US troops in Vietnam in advance and just waiting for a suitable incident to get Congress and the public on their side? Historian Dr William Michael Hammond notes that 'President Johnson's advisers were deeply concerned and during July 1964 began to draft a congressional resolution sanctioning American attacks on North Vietnam as a means of stemming the communist tide.' This was before the Gulf of Tonkin incident occurred. Others feel that Johnson was considering, but had not committed himself to, escalating the war and sending US combat troops until the incident occurred. Vivienne Sanders writes that 'While Johnson was trying to decide whether there had been a second attack, the press reported the supposed incident and Johnson felt trapped, fearing that if he did nothing, his opponent in the presidential election [in November 1964] would call him a coward.'

Dr William Michael Hammond (contributor), *The Vietnam War* (Salamander, 1987); Vivienne Sanders, *The USA and Vietnam* (Hodder & Stoughton, 2002)

3 The Height of Battle

Despite being given wide-ranging military powers by the Gulf of Tonkin Resolution, Johnson and his advisers chose not to send in large numbers of ground troops immediately. Instead they launched some air attacks, increased the numbers of military advisers and made further attempts to bolster the South Vietnamese army, the ARVN. But the ARVN's elite troops were subject to a series of damaging defeats in December 1964. When the Viet Cong attacked US barracks in Pleiku in February 1965, killing eight Americans and wounding over 100, American leaders decided to change their plans.

An invasion of North Vietnam was considered far too dangerous as it could lead to a situation similar to the Korean War and might provoke China or the Soviet Union into sending troops to defend North Vietnam. A massive, extended bombing campaign of North Vietnam was chosen instead in the belief that the United States Air Force (USAF) could harness its immense technological advantage to damage the North Vietnamese economy enough for North Vietnam to halt its support of the communists in South Vietnam.

Sustained Bombing Raids

On 2 March 1965, Operation Rolling Thunder began. It consisted of regular, heavy bombing raids on North Vietnam and communist strongholds in parts of South Vietnam. Some of the aircraft flew from

A US McDonnell-Douglas F4C Phantom flies a low-level bombing raid over a suspected Viet Cong village hideout. The two-seater jet could carry up to 16,000 pounds of bombs, rockets or missiles in a range of combinations. Hundreds of Phantoms saw service in the Vietnam War. Some aircraft were equipped as bombers or fighters, while others flew reconnaissance missions.

Yankee Station, the codename for aircraft carriers in the South China Sea. Others flew from South Vietnam or from airbases in Thailand. The bombing was intended to last approximately eight weeks. In the end, it continued for almost three and a half years, during which time over one million tonnes of bombs were dropped.

Six days after Rolling Thunder's start, the first publicly declared combat troops, a detachment of some 3,500 US Marines, arrived in South Vietnam. The bombing and the dispatch of troops were presented to the US public as being a short-term measure, and support for the action was high in the United States. The bombing was halted briefly in May as the United States tried to start peace talks with North Vietnam but were unsuccessful. A similar attempt was made in December 1965 but was similarly unsuccessful, and bombing resumed in February 1966.

US Marines march through the sand in full battle gear as they land at Da Nang in March 1965, part of some 3,500 marines who formed the first detachment of combat-ready troops to arrive in Vietnam. Da Nang is located approximately halfway between Hanoi to the north and Saigon to the south.

TURNING POINT

Operation Rolling Thunder (1965–68)

Operation Rolling Thunder marked a major change in US military tactics and an obvious escalation in US military activity in Vietnam. The US military was initially confident that a massive, prolonged series of bombing raids carried out by the world's most powerful air force against North Vietnam would be a success. It was intended to demonstrate America's determination to pursue the fight to a conclusion, as well as crushing North Vietnam's industry and damaging the morale of its population. However, North Vietnam was not an industrial society and it lacked large numbers of major industrial targets. In addition, certain key targets, especially those close to the Chinese border, were avoided for fear of drawing China into the conflict. During the Rolling Thunder operation over 640,000 tonnes of bombs were dropped on North Vietnam. While they caused considerable damage and suffering, the bombing did not force North Vietnam to give up fighting and enter into meaningful peace talks.

Away from the bombing, both sides launched propaganda campaigns. The South Vietnamese and Americans depicted the war as self-defence with the US helping a free nation defend itself from attack by a hostile neighbour intent on invasion. The US sought to present the actions of the NLF and Viet Cong as those of communists under orders from and completely controlled by the North Vietnamese government. The North Vietnamese, by contrast, portrayed their support as non-military and declared that the conflict was a civil war between rebels who had the support of most South Vietnamese against a corrupt South Vietnam government that was just a puppet of the United States.

On the ground, the NLF responded to the bombing during Operation Rolling Thunder by focusing their attacks on US military air bases in South Vietnam. General William C. Westmoreland, who had been the commander of US forces in Vietnam since the middle of 1964, argued that the small number of soldiers under his command were nowhere near enough to defend the air bases from attack. Greater numbers of US combat troops began to arrive in South Vietnam and by the end of 1965 Westmoreland had an estimated 180,000-strong force under his command. Soldiers from Australia, Thailand, New Zealand, the Philippines and South Korea eventually joined the force. Two of America's stoutest Cold War allies, Canada and the UK, refused to send troops, although an estimated 30,000 Canadians signed up to serve in the US military during the war.

Commander of the US forces in Vietnam, General William Westmoreland, inspects the 1st Infantry Division in 1965. One of the first divisions of ground troops to arrive in Vietnam, this unit lost over 3,000 soldiers killed in action before the division was recalled to the United States in 1970.

Differing Tactics

The early arrivals in Vietnam were instructed to defend ports, bases and roads, but soon Westmoreland employed more aggressive tactics, known as 'search and destroy'. US forces sought out North Vietnamese army (NVA) units operating in South Vietnam and strongholds of the Viet Cong. Once the enemy was found, the Americans would call in reinforcements and further forces. These

often included helicopters and aircraft carrying troops, heavy artillery and squadrons of bomber aircraft.

The United States planned to use its military and industrial strength to control the seas around Vietnam and the airspace above the country. It fielded large squadrons of aircraft to bomb known communist supply routes and other targets and to obtain supremacy in the air. It took advantage of the latest advances in radar, electronics and 'smart' weapons that could be automatically locked onto their targets.

On the ground, the United States largely sought to fight a conventional war focusing on big battles in which its military forces could employ its superior weaponry. It believed that in major pitched battles, US weaponry and military personnel would be more than a match for the enemy. In November 1965, the first major ground battle involving US troops appeared to prove this belief right. A short, yet fierce, battle in Ia Drang Valley resulted in a

US Army Air Cavalry land in the South Vietnamese countryside after being transported to their target by Bell UH-1 Huey helicopters. A workhorse of US armed forces, the Huey was used mainly as a troop transporter or as a medical air ambulance. Over 2,500 Hueys were lost in operational accidents or through enemy fire in the course of the war.

resounding victory for the Americans, who lost less than 250 personnel while killing an estimated 1,800 NVA soldiers.

However, battles like Ia Drang proved the exception. The US military found it difficult to uncover the Viet Cong and NVA and draw them into large-scale pitched battles. This was principally because the enemy rarely fought as large, easily-detectable units. The Viet Cong, in particular, were hard to locate and pin down as they were organized into very small groups, called cells, of between three and ten people. These small cells of Viet Cong concentrated on attacking small patrols or poorly guarded positions. To increase its advantage, the Viet Cong tended to move and attack at night.

Jungle Warfare

The Viet Cong's guerrilla warfare techniques had been refined by many years of conflict against the Japanese, French and South Vietnamese. Their tactics were well suited to the territory of Vietnam which was characterized by hills, forests and large areas of boggy ground. This sort of terrain was unsuitable for large military vehicles, such as tanks, but was ideal for

Total US Military Personnel in Vietnam

Date	Total Personnel
31 December 1960	900
31 December 1961	3,200
31 December 1962	11,500
31 December 1963	16,300
31 December 1964	23,300
31 December 1965	184,300
31 December 1966	425,300
31 December 1967	485,600
31 December 1968	536,100
31 December 1969	474,400
31 December 1970	335,800
9 June 1971	250,900

Source: Global Security

VOICES FROM THE PAST

Counterproductive tactics

While the Viet Cong sought to win the support of the rural villagers of South Vietnam, the ARVN and American forces that searched for Viet Cong units often treated villagers harshly if any evidence of the Viet Cong was found. One US Marine, William Ehrhart recounted:

'...they'd be beaten pretty badly, maybe tortured. Or they might be hauled off to jail, and God knows what happened to them. At the end of the day, the villagers would be turned loose. Their homes had been wrecked, their chickens killed, their rice confiscated – and if they weren't pro-Viet Cong before we got there, they sure as hell were by the time we left.'

William D. Ehrhart, *Busted: A Vietnam Veteran* (University of Massachusetts Press, 1995)

American heavy artillery pounds a Viet Cong location during April 1968. The American reliance on heavy firepower both on the ground and in the air did score some notable individual victories but never secured South Vietnam outright.

This map shows the major engagements between 1965 and 1967 in South Vietnam. The winding Ho Chi Minh system of trails was used to ferry people, arms and supplies from North Vietnam into strategic points in South Vietnam.

stealthy attacks on foot by small groups carrying rifles, machine guns, mortars, grenades and small bombs. Using their greater knowledge of the terrain, the Viet Cong were able to attack and harass American and South Vietnamese targets or to lay secret booby traps. Some were pits filled with sharpened sticks that were concealed by a covering layer of foliage. Other traps triggered explosives with devastating effect. After laying booby traps or attacking a target, the Viet Cong would retreat deep into the jungle or into hideouts, such as tunnels, or disappear into rural villages that were sympathetic to the communists.

Part of the Viet Cong plan was to gain the support of more and more ordinary villagers. Successive South Vietnamese governments had done little to improve the life of peasants in the villages, most of whom were poor, owned no land and had to work for landowners. When the Viet Cong took control of a village or area, they often dismissed or executed the landlords and divided the land amongst the peasants.

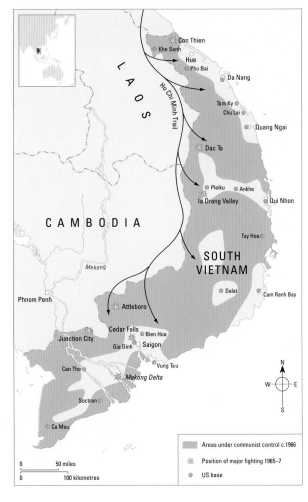

Con Thien
Khe Sanh
Hue
Phu Bai
Da Nang
LAOS
Ho Chi Minh Trail
Tam Ky
Chu Lai
Quang Ngai
Dac To
Pleiku   Ankhe
Ia Drang Valley   Qui Nhon
CAMBODIA
Tuy Hoa
SOUTH VIETNAM
Mekong
Dalat   Cam Ranh Bay
Phnom Penh   Attleboro
Cedar Falls
Junction City   Bien Hoa
Gia Dinh   Saigon
Can Tho
Vung Tau
Mekong Delta
Soctran
Ca Mau

0   50 miles
0   100 kilometres

Areas under communist control c.1966
Position of major fighting 1965–7
US base

A young US soldier sits warily in his encampment deep in the Vietnamese jungle with only a skull wedged between branches for company. The stresses and strains of fighting an unknown enemy who used hit-and-run tactics and surviving in an alien environment took its toll on many American soldiers.

This made them popular with many village people from whose numbers they gathered new recruits to their forces. Villages that resisted or opposed the communists were often attacked and destroyed.

The Viet Cong and its supporters were used to living in the climate, conditions and terrain found in Vietnam. Large numbers of their personnel had been fighting using guerrilla tactics for many years and were highly experienced. By contrast, the average age of the American soldier in Vietnam was just nineteen. Many US soldiers were very inexperienced and had never before left the safety of the United States to make a tour of duty in a foreign country.

Lack of Experience

The inexperience of the American troops was compounded by the shortness of their tours of duty, most of which only lasted one year. By the time soldiers had built up valuable experience fighting in Vietnam, they were sent back to the United States. New arrivals in Vietnam were rarely trusted by battle-hardened veterans. This led to the new recruits being isolated or given the most dangerous tasks by more experienced soldiers.

VOICES FROM THE PAST

Fear of the unknown

The mainly young US ground troops often could not tell friend from foe or predict where and when the next attack would come from. US Marine Captain E. J. Banks recalled:

'You never knew who was the enemy and who was your friend. They all looked alike. They all dressed alike. They were all Vietnamese. Some of them were Viet Cong. Here's a woman...she tells an interrogator that...she isn't Viet Cong. But she watches your men walk down a trail and get killed or wounded by a booby trap. She knows the booby trap is there, but she doesn't warn them. Maybe, she planted it herself.'

Captain E. J. Banks quoted in Stanley Karnow, Vietnam: A History (Penguin, 1991)

Many American ground troops, barely out of school, found the unfamiliar language, people and surroundings hard to cope with. They suffered from the intense heat and humidity of Vietnam's climate, and from mosquito bites and tropical diseases, such as malaria and dysentery. Many more suffered from low morale and deep fear of the communists' style of guerrilla fighting. In the past American soldiers had been used to fighting an easily identifiable enemy. In Vietnam, they could not tell which Vietnamese were friendly and which were foes.

Striving for Control

The number of US and allied troops who were committed to this unfamiliar theatre of war increased throughout 1966 and 1967, but the pattern of warfare remained the same. The communists would engage in hit-and-run attacks. The Americans would respond with search and destroy missions. On several occasions, US troops won victories over communist forces in an area, but they were unable to gain complete control of the region.

Armoured personnel carriers take part in the destruction of vegetation around a Viet Cong stronghold called the Iron Triangle only 50 km away from Saigon. The mission, codenamed Operation Cedar Falls, involved some 16,000 US and 14,000 ARVN troops. A massive tunnel system was discovered full of Viet Cong equipment and supplies.

To try to help gain control over rural regions, the US forces sought to remove the enemy's hiding places and to destroy the routes along which arms and other supplies were transported. Supply routes were bombed and US aircraft dropped increasingly large quantities of chemicals called defoliants that stripped trees and bushes of their leaves. US forces bulldozed and destroyed networks of tunnels, swathes of forest and even villages that were sympathetic to the Viet

Cong. Yet, despite these activities and the increasingly heavy losses that the communists suffered, the Viet Cong and NVA continued to receive reinforcements and supplies.

In 1967, as Viet Cong and NVA losses mounted heavily, some US political and military leaders began to believe that the course of the war might be turning in their favour. However, the Tet Offensive of 1968 marked a major change in the fortunes of both sides as it helped to persuade more and more American people, some of them in high office in the United States, that the war was essentially unwinnable.

US Marines in full battle dress wait to move up to Khe Sanh as reinforcements during the North Vietnamese siege of the American base there in 1968. The 6,000 US soldiers at Khe Sanh managed to hold out during the 77-day siege, assisted by extremely heavy aerial bombardment delivered by American aircraft and helicopter gunships.

Khe Sanh and The Tet Offensive

At the beginning of 1968, the North Vietnamese government decided to embark on a massive military campaign. NVA troops and Viet Cong guerrillas were readied and the campaign began with a massed attack on and siege of a 6,000-strong US military base at Khe Sanh. The base was an important one for the Americans, and the North Vietnamese hoped that their attack would draw US attention away

TURNING POINT
The Tet Offensive

The Tet Offensive was an undoubted military failure for the Viet Cong and the North Vietnamese Army. Losses were huge, little territory was gained and the expected uprising of South Vietnamese in the cities and towns did not occur. Yet, by providing evidence to senior US politicians, generals and the general public that the war was either far from being won or perhaps even unwinnable, it proved a major turning point in the conflict. As former North Vietnamese colonel Bui Tin wrote, 'Our losses were staggering and a complete surprise. Giap later told me that Tet had been a military defeat, though we gained the planned political advantages.'

Bui Tin, *Following Ho Chi Minh* (University of Hawaii Press, 1999)

HOW DID IT HAPPEN?

Fighting the wrong war?

Did the United States simply make the mistake of fighting the wrong type of war in Vietnam? Historian Douglas Pike argues that 'the American military's performance was particularly impressive. It won every significant battle fought, a record virtually unparalleled in the history of warfare.'

Others, such as Andrew Krepinevich, maintain that America did fight the wrong sort of war in Vietnam, not concerning itself enough with the political struggle waged by the Viet Cong to win over South Vietnamese and not developing the skills to fight rebels such as 'long-term patrolling of a small area, the pervasive use of night operations, emphasis on intelligence on the insurgents', instead opting for 'conventional war and a reliance on high volumes of firepower'.

Douglas Pike, *PAVN: People's Army of Vietnam* (Da Capo Press, 1991); Andrew Krepinevich, *The Army and Vietnam* (Johns Hopkins University Press, 1986)

A US serviceman walks through the battle-scarred streets of Hue in the aftermath of successful American efforts to repel the NVA from the city. The street fighting in Hue in the early months of 1968 resulted in US casualties of around 1,000 soldiers either killed or wounded.

from other regions where they planned to mount their major offensive. This was launched on Tet Nguyen Dan, the Lunar New Year (30-31 January 1968), a traditional holiday in Vietnam.

Giap and his generals gambled on winning a major, and potentially decisive, victory by abandoning guerrilla techniques in favour of open battle pursued with the element of surprise. The communists also hoped that such a show of strength would cause sympathisers in South Vietnam to rise up and join their forces in large numbers. An estimated 85,000 Viet Cong and NVA began attacks on 100 of South Vietnam's towns and cities. Because over 40 percent of the South Vietnamese army was on holiday leave, the Tet Offensive was successful at first as the communists drove deep into many major cities including Hue and Saigon. In Hue, they repelled enemy forces for over a month, during which they hunted down and killed between 3,000 and 6,000 South Vietnamese government supporters. Elsewhere, though, savage fighting drove the communists back out of most towns and cities within one or two weeks with huge losses. The siege of Khe Sanh lasted until 8 April when a US force broke the deadlock. Altogether the communists lost between 45,000 and 58,000 troops at Khe Sanh and during the Tet Offensive.

4 Mounting Opposition

By the time of the Tet Offensive, a major anti-war movement was building in the United States. It had started as early as 1964–65, primarily in colleges and universities where a number of lecturers and students were actively making their opposition known. Some were unhappy about the United States supporting a harsh South Vietnamese government, and some were pacifists (against all wars). Others believed that America was in the war principally to serve its own economic ends by exploiting Vietnam's raw materials, and those of other south-east Asian countries, and by selling them US-made goods.

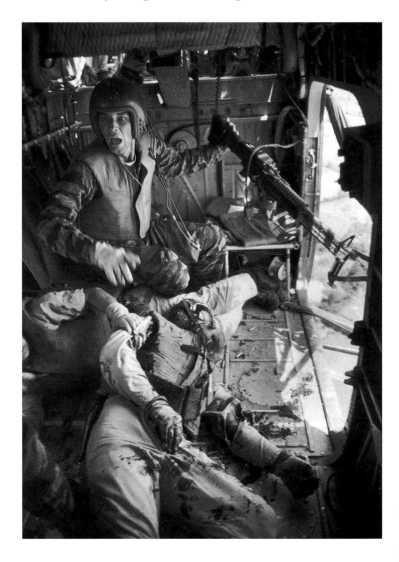

Lance Corporal James Farley calls for assistance as he crouches over the injured pilot of another helicopter that Farley's crew had helped to rescue. The pilot, James Magel, died before the helicopter reached a medical unit. This scene was captured by award-winning photojournalist Larry Burrows, who was himself shot down and killed in a helicopter flying over Laos in 1971.

VOICES FROM THE PAST

Critic inside the government

Undersecretary of State George Ball was one of the few voices within Johnson's administration opposed to continuing the war. In 1966, in memos to the president, he wrote:

'From our point of view, the terrain in South Viet-Nam could not be worse. Jungles and rice paddies are not designed for modern arms... Politically, South Viet-Nam is a lost cause. The country is bled white from twenty years of war and the people are sick of it... Hanoi has a Government and a purpose and a discipline. The "government" in Saigon is a travesty... If ever there was an occasion for a tactical withdrawal, this is it.'

US Department of State S/S Files Lot 70 D 48

A CBS TV news reporter, Dan Rather, broadcasts a report back to the United States. The war was the first major conflict to be heavily televised and the graphic TV footage of events in Vietnam influenced some people in the United States and elsewhere around the world to adopt an anti-war stance.

Nevertheless, during the mid-1960s the majority of the American people supported Johnson's actions in Vietnam and believed in the domino theory. At this time the United States government portrayed the conflict as a limited war, within strict boundaries, that they would not let escalate into a war between the superpowers. The American population were fearful of communism and generally supported American attempts to prevent it from spreading to more countries. Many people were confident that America's military might would ensure a relatively rapid end to the conflict and they were proud of their country's leading role in the fight against communism.

Changing Public Opinion

As the war progressed without an obvious victory, however, anti-war sentiment began to increase in the United States. Troop numbers in Vietnam rose sharply and so did casualties. Between 1961 and 1965, the United States lost 1,864 personnel killed in action. In 1966 alone, it lost 6,000, and in 1967 over 11,000. More young Americans were drafted into military service. For their families and communities, this turned the war from being something remote to being something extremely personal.

The US Air Force tests napalm at Elgin Airfield in Florida. Napalm was first developed by American scientists at Harvard University during the Second World War. A mixture of petroleum and a thickening agent, it was propelled by flamethrowers or incendiary bombs and once it started burning, was very difficult to extinguish. It was used extensively in the Vietnam War to draw Viet Cong and NVA troops out of dense vegetation by burning it down.

Television, which had recently established itself as a global mass medium, gave the public greater access to information about the war than had been the case for any previous conflict. Opposition to the war began to mount as journalists' reports and TV footage revealed the casualties suffered not only by American soldiers and their allies, but also by civilians caught up in the fighting throughout South Vietnam. Many were horrified by the use of weapons such as napalm, an inflammable liquid that consumes skin, flesh and muscle. The human suffering in Vietnam was not the only issue that concerned the American media and public. Many people were unhappy about the rising cost of the war (believed to be as much as US$20 billion in 1968, for example) and the increase in taxes, as well as cuts in welfare programmes, that were necessary to fund it.

One figure inside the White House who had become increasingly sceptical of America's participation in the war was US Secretary of Defense Robert McNamara, a close adviser to Johnson. McNamara was influenced by his son and daughter, who both demonstrated at anti-war protests, and by a growing belief that the country could not win the war. In November 1967, McNamara's resignation as secretary of defense was announced.

Public opinion was further influenced when, two months later, the Tet Offensive was launched and pictures of the savage fighting were broadcast on television screens around the world. Prior to Tet, a number of US military and political leaders had assured the US public that the war would shortly be over. After Tet, increasing numbers of Americans doubted this to be true. While active anti-war protesters were still a relatively small minority, many more people blamed their president for continuing the war or for waging it in the wrong way. Johnson's approval rating in opinion polls dropped and he started to suffer ill health. On 31 March 1968, he announced he would not run for a second term as US president.

Anti-war protesters burn their draft cards during a 1967 demonstration in Washington D.C. Issues and controversies about the draft rumbled on in the United States throughout the Vietnam War. Some people believed that the draft was biased because fewer middle-class, wealthy Americans were drafted to serve in Vietnam than were members of poorer ethnic minorities.

'Peace With Honor'

The presidential election in November 1968 was dominated by the issue of the Vietnam War. The winner, Republican Richard Nixon, had maintained during his election campaign that he would seek 'peace with honor'. The electorate was deeply divided. On one side stood a growing anti-war movement who pointed to mounting casualties. On the other hand, the majority of the US population continued to support US troops in Vietnam. They believed that America was fighting a just war to prevent a communist takeover of a free country. Reports of communist atrocities, especially the murders of civilians, were seized upon as proof that the communists had to be stopped and that the South Vietnamese needed protection by American forces.

This view was shaken when reports of atrocities committed by America's own soldiers reached the United States. News of the My

TURNING POINT
My Lai massacre

News of a massacre of civilians by US troops outraged many ordinary Americans in 1969 and increased public anti-war sentiment. In March 1968, US soldiers landed by helicopter in Song My, a well-known Viet Cong area that included My Lai and several other villages. They were given instructions to trap and execute any opposition they encountered. The platoon of soldiers, led by Lieutenant William Calley, found only women, children and elderly men in the area, and encountered no enemy fire, yet they burned down My Lai and killed 357 people there, along with 150 more in nearby hamlets. The army covered up the massacre and it was only a year later that a soldier serving in another unit heard about the incident, and contacted his congressman. The *New York Times* broke the story and the public was outraged and sickened by the atrocities. Investigations into the massacre dragged on into 1971 when Calley was sentenced to life imprisonment. Many Americans were split about his sentencing as some considered him a scapegoat. Calley was pardoned three and a half years later by President Richard Nixon.

A US soldier fans the flames of a fire holding a basket used to dry rice and root crops. The fire is burning in the village of My Lai, the scene of one of the worst atrocities performed by US troops during the Vietnam War. When news of the carnage at My Lai emerged, it caused outrage around the world.

Lai massacre shocked public opinion when it broke in 1969. It helped lead to growth in the protest organization Vietnam Veterans Against the War (VVAW). This group, which was founded in 1967, filmed around 100 veterans testifying that atrocities like those committed at My Lai had occurred throughout the war, even if they were not on quite the same horrific scale.

Major Protests

The VVAW was just one of many anti-war groups that grew in strength between 1967 and 1969. As anti-war sentiment grew, protests and demonstrations became larger and more frequent. On 15 October 1969, hundreds of thousands of people took part in National Moratorium anti-war demonstrations across the United States. A second round of similar demonstrations occurred exactly a month later, with over a quarter of a million people demonstrating in Washington D.C. Protesters increasingly came from all walks of life and had differing reasons for opposing the continuation of the war. Some were appalled at the human suffering or the financial cost of the war. Others felt that the war was not winnable, or that US troops should no longer fight someone else's war. Whatever their reasons, it was clear that opposition to the war was becoming hard for the US government to ignore.

Veterans of the Vietnam War join forces with peace protesters at a demonstration in Washington D.C. in 1971. A group of veterans camped in the National Mall park in Washington for a week in protest at the war, while 50 veterans attempted to turn themselves in to the military authorities in the Pentagon as war criminals for taking part in a war that they now felt was wrong and unlawful.

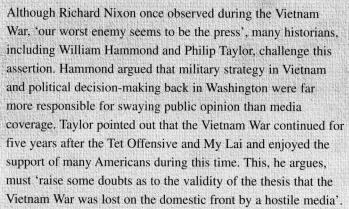

HOW DID IT HAPPEN?

Did the media lose America the war?

Although Richard Nixon once observed during the Vietnam War, 'our worst enemy seems to be the press', many historians, including William Hammond and Philip Taylor, challenge this assertion. Hammond argued that military strategy in Vietnam and political decision-making back in Washington were far more responsible for swaying public opinion than media coverage. Taylor pointed out that the Vietnam War continued for five years after the Tet Offensive and My Lai and enjoyed the support of many Americans during this time. This, he argues, must 'raise some doubts as to the validity of the thesis that the Vietnam War was lost on the domestic front by a hostile media'.

Media scholar and historian Marshall McLuhan, however, opposed this view, stating in 1975 that 'television brought the brutality of war into the comfort of the living room. Vietnam was lost in the living rooms of America – not on the battlefields of Vietnam.'

William Hammond, *Reporting Vietnam: Media and Military at War* (University Press of Kansas, 1999); Philip M. Taylor, *Munitions of the Mind* 3rd Edition (Manchester University Press, 2003); Marshall McLuhan, *Montreal Gazette* article, May 1975

5 The Long Road to Peace

In 1969, the year of the National Moratorium demonstrations and Nixon's first year in office, US force numbers in Vietnam reached their peak of about 540,000. In June of that year Nixon announced the withdrawal of 25,000 troops. Peace talks began in secret in August 1969 and a further 65,000 troops were shipped back to the United States by the end of the year. Troop numbers dropped significantly in each of the following three years. By the end of 1971, American forces in Vietnam numbered 140,000.

Despite a gradual reduction in troop numbers, US casualties continued to mount and anti-war opposition grew and grew. It was spurred on by revelations of more atrocities and sinking morale among US soldiers, which led to record numbers of desertions or attacks by soldiers on their own officers. Then, in 1970, US forces invaded Cambodia seeking to destroy Viet Cong bases and supply routes in that country. This provoked

An American armoured personnel carrier drives past two dead Cambodians during the incursion by US forces into Cambodia. American troops entered Cambodia in April 1970 to support the new regime of the pro-American leader, General Lon Nol. But the incursion aroused great hostility at home and the US Congress ordered President Nixon to withdraw US ground troops from Cambodia by the end of June 1970.

TURNING POINT

Publication of the Pentagon Papers

One event that triggered intense anti-war protest amongst the media and public was the publication of the Pentagon Papers. These top secret documents charted US interest and involvement in Vietnam since the 1940s. The *New York Times* newspaper began publishing them in 1971. They showed how politicians and military leaders in previous US governments had sometimes lied or covered up incidents during the war. Nixon tried to stop their publication but the Supreme Court allowed them to be published. Many Americans were shocked at how their government had acted. Anti-war sentiment grew as more demonstrators and protesters took to the streets.

VOICES FROM THE PAST

Nixon and South Vietnamese self-reliance

Nixon and his advisers stated that they sought an honourable way out of the war which would leave South Vietnam secure and American prestige intact. Nixon appealed to Americans that:

The nation's objective should be to help the South Vietnamese fight the war and not fight it for them. If they do not assume the majority of the burden in their own defense, they cannot be saved.'

President Richard Nixon quoted in Stephen Ambrose, *Nixon: The Triumph of A Politician* (Simon & Schuster, 1989)

North Vietnamese soldiers assault a paratroop base in Laos during fierce fighting in 1971. The invasion of Laos to seek out and destroy NVA troops and bases was carried out by ARVN ground troops. Despite mixed success for the ARVN, President Nixon told America in an April 1971 television address that the operations showed 'without American advisers they [the ARVN] could fight effectively against the best troops North Vietnam could put in the field. Consequently, I can report tonight that Vietnamization has succeeded.'

more outrage from a world fearing a 'second Vietnam'. The invasion achieved little and US troops withdrew after two months.

Vietnamization

In 1971 another major operation outside Vietnam's borders was conducted in Laos. It too was intended to seek out communist forces and to attack their supply routes. This time it was carried out solely by South Vietnam's own army, the ARVN. A change in policy had occurred. This policy, known as Vietnamization, had been developed by Nixon and his secretary of state Henry Kissinger. It was designed to create a strong, self-reliant South Vietnam that would allow the US eventually to withdraw all of its troops. It involved a series of actions, including massive supplies of arms and training to South Vietnamese forces, further pressure imposed on North Vietnam through more bombing raids, and the building of support for the South Vietnamese government now led by Nguyen Van Thieu. By the end of 1972, South Vietnam had the world's fourth largest air force, fourth largest army, and fifth largest navy.

South Vietnamese soldiers congregate around the bodies of two North Vietnamese killed in fighting during the Easter Offensive in 1972. While the NVA losses were heavy and a complete invasion of South Vietnam was prevented, North Vietnam made large gains in South Vietnamese territory.

As well as equipping the South Vietnamese military, the US sought to tackle the Viet Cong on two other fronts. US and ARVN forces began Operation Phoenix to identify and arrest Viet Cong suspects in areas under South Vietnam's control. Although it was brutal and led to the deaths of an estimated 17,000 Vietnamese, Operation Phoenix was considered a tactical success because it removed many communist groups from South Vietnam. The United States also recognized that it had been slow to appreciate the success of the Viet Cong's methods of building support in South Vietnam villages. The US sought to counter this problem by winning over South Vietnamese 'hearts and minds' through public building projects such as bridges, roads, schools and medical centres.

The Easter Offensive Onwards

By the end of 1971, the US policy of Vietnamization was bearing fruit. While the South Vietnamese still relied on the United States for air support, they had accepted responsibility for all combat on the ground. It was not long before the North Vietnamese decided to test

South Vietnam's military prowess and resolve by launching a surprise offensive starting on Easter 1972. Some 130,000 North Vietnamese troops occupied Quang Tri province, and attacked part of the Central Highlands and regions north of Saigon.

The North Vietnamese forces surprised the South Vietnamese by avoiding guerrilla warfare in favour of fighting a conventional war, out in the open, with large numbers of troops, supplies and heavy weaponry. The North Vietnamese forces required large bases and established routes along which to ferry fuel and other vital supplies. US aircraft, now equipped with even more accurate weapons, found the large North Vietnamese forces and their bases and supply routes relatively easy to target from the air. A series of US bombing raids, called Operation Linebacker, devastated North Vietnamese forces and supplies. Nevertheless, the North Vietnamese managed to hold onto large gains they made in South Vietnamese territory during the Easter Offensive.

Progress Towards Peace in Paris

Peace talks, which had been taking place in an on-off fashion since 1969, were given an impetus by the Easter Offensive. Formal talks were held in Paris and attended by representatives of all sides. In addition, Henry Kissinger and North Vietnam's chief negotiator, Le Duc Tho, held secret meetings. In October 1972, a month before the US presidential election, success seemed close at hand. However, the South Vietnamese government, fearing that the US was about to abandon it to a likely takeover by the communists in the north, refused to accept the plan. Nixon was reelected as US president in November and he urged the North Vietnamese to reenter peace negotiations. He also threatened to make an agreement without the South Vietnamese government's co-operation. After the negotiations stalled, Nixon ordered Operation Linebacker II to begin. This bombing campaign, one of the most severe in history, destroyed many

US Secretary of State Henry Kissinger (left) with North Vietnam's chief negotiator, Le Duc Tho, during the Paris Peace Talks in June 1973. The pair were awarded the 1973 Nobel Peace Prize for negotiating a ceasefire in Vietnam. Tho, however, refused the award, as he maintained true peace had not been established.

military targets as well as killing 1,600 civilians. It was halted in January 1973. A peace deal was finally agreed upon a few days later.

The peace agreement was formally signed on 27 January 1973. In it, the United States agreed to withdraw all of its combat troops from Vietnam within 60 days in exchange for the release of American prisoners of war. There would be a ceasefire throughout Indo-China and all personnel would remain only in those areas that they controlled at the time of the ceasefire. In March 1973 the North Vietnamese released 691 American prisoners, mostly captured aircrew. On 29 March, the last of America's fighting forces, their ground troops, left South Vietnam leaving only military trainers and support staff behind.

Uncertain Times for Thieu

Sporadic, localized fighting occurred throughout 1973. The South Vietnamese made small gains, but Thieu feared that after the Americans had left, and with the North Vietnamese in control of parts of South Vietnam, it would not be long before the North Vietnamese attempted to make further inroads into South Vietnam. Thieu had obtained a written assurance from Nixon that America would continue to support South Vietnam and would send in troops if North Vietnam broke the peace agreement by invading. However, in 1974 Nixon resigned from office and the US Congress passed a law that meant that a president could no longer send troops abroad without the approval of Congress. Congress at that time was strongly opposed to reentering the Vietnam conflict.

As part of the peace agreement signed in 1973, both sides agreed to return all captured military personnel within 60 days. Here, some NVA prisoners are given a welcome return by fellow North Vietnamese. The fate of a number of US serviceman believed captured but not returned remained a major political issue between the United States and Vietnam for many years.

The United States also slashed its military aid to South Vietnam, reducing it to $1.1 billion in 1974, less than half the level of the previous year. The South Vietnamese economy was struggling and with less US aid, the ARVN was crippled by a lack of funds. Fuel ran low, spare parts and ammunition dried up and the morale of troops fell further. Many soldiers were not paid enough even to feed

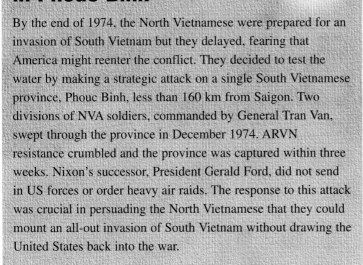

TURNING POINT

Testing US response in Phouc Binh

By the end of 1974, the North Vietnamese were prepared for an invasion of South Vietnam but they delayed, fearing that America might reenter the conflict. They decided to test the water by making a strategic attack on a single South Vietnamese province, Phouc Binh, less than 160 km from Saigon. Two divisions of NVA soldiers, commanded by General Tran Van, swept through the province in December 1974. ARVN resistance crumbled and the province was captured within three weeks. Nixon's successor, President Gerald Ford, did not send in US forces or order heavy air raids. The response to this attack was crucial in persuading the North Vietnamese that they could mount an all-out invasion of South Vietnam without drawing the United States back into the war.

ARVN armoured vehicles patrol a road in South Vietnam. With the reduction in military aid from the US, South Vietnam's military forces, left to fend for themselves without US ground troops, experienced shortages in supplies and fuel. The ARVN was a large, modern army that cost almost three billion dollars a year to run. When aid was slashed, the South Vietnamese government struggled to finance its forces.

VOICES FROM THE PAST

Thieu resigns

Thieu resigned as South Vietnamese leader in a 90-minute-long radio and TV broadcast. In it, he criticized the Americans for going back on their promises:

'At the time of the peace agreement the United States agreed to replace equipment on a one-by-one basis...But the United States did not keep its word. Is an American's word reliable these days? The United States did not keep its promise to help us fight for freedom and it was in the same fight that the United States lost 50,000 of its young men.'

BBC TV archive

An NVA tank crashes through the gates of the Presidential Palace in Saigon on 30 April 1975. The capture of the palace in the heart of South Vietnam's capital city marked the end of South Vietnam as a separate state. The two Vietnams were formally reunited during the following year.

their families. In contrast, North Vietnam slowly replenished its forces and by the end of 1974 was in a position to launch an attack. The first target was Phouc Binh province, and this assault was followed by a general offensive in South Vietnam.

The Final Push

The North Vietnamese began this attack in March 1975 and advanced rapidly. The city of Hue was captured on 26 March and Da Nang, south of Hue, fell three days later. Thieu ordered his troops to retreat from the Central Highlands southwards so that they could regroup and defend Saigon and the south. It proved a disastrous move. The NVA harried the retreating ARVN and the few routes south from the Central Highlands became jammed with troops and fleeing civilians who were fired upon repeatedly by NVA artillery. It is estimated that over 100,000 people died or were captured. The remaining ARVN in the very north of South Vietnam were cut off and were defeated rapidly. In the south of the country, NVA troops advanced to surround Saigon. The atmosphere amongst the South Vietnamese was one of panic.

When Thieu resigned as South Vietnamese leader on 21 April, the North Vietnamese sensed outright victory and pressed on to capture Saigon. The remaining US personnel in the country organized a last-minute evacuation and airlifted an estimated 50,000 people out of Saigon before NVA tanks crashed through the gates of the Presidential Palace. The final surrender of the South Vietnamese government was accepted on 30 April 1975. In 1976, the two halves of Vietnam were formally reunited and the country was renamed the Socialist Republic of Vietnam; Saigon became Ho Chi Minh City.

In Ruins

While the war was over, the devastation and suffering were not. The war had left as many as five million dead and hundreds of thousands wounded. Amongst the Vietnam population in 1975 were an estimated 879,000 orphans. The country's industry, schools, transport links and sanitation systems lay in rubble. Chemical defoliants and mines had ruined much of the country's farmland, and famines and food shortages would affect Vietnam for the next 15 years. Chemicals found in one commonly-used defoliant, Agent Orange, were later proved to cause cancer.

The devastation wrought by the chemical Agent Orange is apparent in this defoliated area at Binhtre in South Vietnam. Agent Orange was just one of a number of herbicides sprayed by the US and South Vietnamese forces to remove jungle cover concealing the communist forces and to destroy their crops. Over 86 million litres of herbicide were dispersed in South Vietnam between 1961 and 1970.

As many in South Vietnam feared, the communists instituted a harsh regime. Some 60,000 South Vietnamese government and army members and supporters of the war against communism were executed and thousands more were sent to prison camps. Around a million Vietnamese were resettled, mostly moving from South Vietnam's cities into the countryside. Some minority groups were persecuted, particularly the Chinese in Vietnam, many of whom were relatively wealthy. They were stripped of their wealth and Chinese newspapers and schools were forcibly closed. Despite the assistance

These Vietnamese boat people have managed to arrive at Hong Kong in 1979 after a perilous journey from their homeland across the South China Sea. Many Vietnamese who tried to escape their country in this way perished on the voyage.

China had given to North Vietnam during the early stages of the conflict, relations between the two countries had deteriorated. In 1979 China even attempted to invade Vietnam.

Life under communist rule was hard and an estimated 1.5 million Vietnamese 'boat people' fled the country in the late 1970s by stowing away onboard foreign ships or taking to sea in flimsy boats and rafts. Many perished en route while thousands more arrived as refugees in other countries in south-east Asia.

The impact of the war on Vietnam had been immense. No one is certain of the exact figures but it is estimated that between 150,000 and 225,000 members of the South Vietnamese Army were killed, and as many as double that number severely injured. As many as 1.1 million North Vietnamese and Vietcong were dead and 600,000 wounded. In addition, over one million Vietnamese civilians were killed. The Americans lost 47,000 personnel killed in combat and a further 11,000 from other causes such as disease. America's allies also suffered casualties: South Korea lost 4,500, Australia over 500 and Thailand 350.

The American Experience

The Vietnam War created issues that affected American politics for many years after the war's end. The United States' image as a global military and political superpower had been damaged by the conflict, which had cost the nation over $120 billion and had deeply divided its society. The war affected American foreign policy – the country avoided sending large numbers of troops into any conflict for almost two decades, until the 1991 Gulf War. Issues surrounding the war continued to generate public debate in the United States and to make the headlines. Many families campaigned to learn the fate of American personnel labelled as missing in action (MIA) and the issue of the treatment of the returning Vietnam veterans also aroused debate. Many thousands of the three million Americans who had served during the Vietnam War found it extremely hard to reintegrate into society. Some suffered from disabilities or post-traumatic stress disorder, and others committed suicide. To this day, the Vietnam War continues to divide opinion amongst historians, military figures and the general public.

HOW DID IT HAPPEN?

Who let down whom?

Were the South Vietnamese betrayed and abandoned by the United States or did the South Vietnamese, well-equipped by the US, fail to defend themselves? Nixon maintained that 'In early 1973, when we left South Vietnam, we left it in a strong position militarily… We had tried to tip the balance of power toward the South Vietnamese by launching a massive re-supply effort in late 1972.'

Others point out that the force with which the US equipped South Vietnam was too expensive for the South Vietnamese to run, and maintain that the massive cuts in aid and political negotiations between America and North Vietnam undermined and abandoned South Vietnam. Historian Ian Beckett writes that 'Nixon's only real aim was to withdraw US troops with honour and little was done to ensure the future security of South Vietnam.'

Richard Nixon, *No More Vietnams* (Arbor House Publishing, 1987); Ian Beckett, *Southeast Asia From 1945* (Franklin Watts, 1986)

US president Ronald Reagan and his wife, Nancy, stand by the Vietnam Memorial in Washington D.C. Designed by a 22-year-old architectural student, Maya Ying Lin, the two black granite walls are carved with the names of 58,183 Americans who lost their lives in the Vietnam War.

Vietnam Timeline

1941 Vietminh formed to fight for Vietnam's independence

1945 Ho Chi Minh declares Vietnam independent and creates provisional government

1949 Communists under Mao Tse-tung take control of China

1954 **May:** Vietminh defeat French at Dien Bien Phu. French rule in Vietnam ends
July: Vietnam is temporarily divided into two nations by the agreements reached at the Geneva Conference

1955 **October:** Bao Dai removed from power in South Vietnam, replaced by Ngo Dinh Diem as South Vietnam's first president

1959 Construction of the Ho Chi Minh trail under way. Guerrilla warfare backed by North Vietnam begins in South Vietnam

1961 US president John F. Kennedy announces increased military aid to South Vietnam

1963 **January:** Viet Cong units defeat South Vietnamese Army (ARVN) in Battle of Ap Bac
1-2 November: South Vietnamese President Diem overthrown and killed
22 November: Kennedy assassinated and succeeded by Lyndon Johnson

1964 **August:** Gulf of Tonkin incident leads to a major escalation of US forces in Vietnam

1965 **February:** Operation Rolling Thunder – the heavy bombing campaign against North Vietnam – begins

1967 **September:** Nguyen Van Thieu wins South Vietnam's presidential election
October: First major anti-war protests in the United States take place in Washington D.C. and elsewhere

1968 **January-February:** North Vietnamese and Viet Cong forces attack South Vietnamese cities in the Tet Offensive
March: My Lai massacre of civilians by US forces. News of the massacre eventually reaches the public the following year causing an outcry
November: Richard Nixon becomes US president succeeding Lyndon Johnson

1969 **April:** US troop levels in Vietnam reach their peak at over 540,000
June: President Nixon announces limited troop withdrawals and begins policy of Vietnamization

1972 **April:** Launch of Easter Offensive by the North Vietnamese army
May: Quang Tri City falls to the North Vietnamese army
December: Heavy bombing of North Vietnam by US aircraft

1973 **27 January:** Peace agreement signed by the United States and North Vietnam

1974 **August:** Richard Nixon resigns and is succeeded as president by Gerald Ford.
December: North Vietnam launches offensive on Phouc Binh province

1975 **30 April:** North Vietnamese capture South Vietnam capital of Saigon. South Vietnam surrenders

1976 Vietnam becomes one country, the Socialist Republic of Vietnam, and Saigon is renamed Ho Chi Minh City

Glossary

ARVN Army of the Republic of Vietnam, the South Vietnamese military forces on the ground.

assassinate To kill a person considered a threat to national security.

civil war A war fought inside the borders of a country by opposing groups. It is usually fought between a government's forces and rebels seeking to overthrow a government.

Cold War Distrustful and hostile relationship between the Soviet Union and its allies and the United States and its allies which developed shortly after the Second World War.

communist Someone who believes in communism, a political system in which the state's property and wealth is owned by the people.

conventional warfare The use of regular armed forces fighting battles in the open with heavy arms and equipment.

coup The overthrow of a government by a small group, often members of the army.

covert Performed in secret.

defoliant A chemical that kill the leaves of trees and plants.

democratic Government that is appointed as a result of free and fair elections.

dictatorship A country run by a single person, a dictator, who has absolute power.

domino theory The notion that if one country in a region were to fall to communism, then other countries would quickly fall to communism as well.

guerrillas Soldiers, not part of a regular army, who use surprise attacks and stay hidden in order to combat an army with greater numbers or superior weaponry.

gunships Aircraft and helicopters fitted with guns and missiles used to attack ground troops.

infiltrate To enter a group or region secretly.

intelligence Information important to a country or group's security, often concerning enemy weapons and troop movements.

NLF National Liberation Front, an organization established in 1960 dedicated to overthrowing the South Vietnamese government. The military arm of the NLF was known as the Viet Cong.

NVA The North Vietnamese Army, also referred to in some texts as the People's Army North Vietnam or PAVN.

propaganda Deliberate methods of communication and influence used to persuade people to believe certain ideas or to behave in a certain way.

reunification The act of bringing a divided country together into one nation.

Viet Cong Term used to describe the communist guerrilla fighters operating in South Vietnam.

Further Information

Books:

Demarco, Neil, *Vietnam 1939–1975* (Hodder & Stoughton, 1998)

Grant, Reg, *Atlas of Conflicts: The Vietnam War* (Franklin Watts, 2004)

Sanders, Vivienne, *Access To History: The USA and Vietnam* (Hodder Headline, 2002)

Wiest, Andrew, *Essential Histories: The Vietnam War* (Osprey, 2002)

Willoughby, David, *20th Century Perspectives: The Vietnam War* (Heinemann, 2001)

Websites:

http://servercc.oakton.edu/~wittman/

http://www.nytimes.com/learning/general/specials/saigon/

http://www.pbs.org/battlefieldvietnam/

http://www.pbs.org/wgbh/amex/vietnam/index.html

http://www.spartacus.schoolnet.co.uk/vietnam.html

http://www.wellesley.edu/Polisci/wj/vietlink.html

Index   Numbers in **bold** refer to pictures

Agent Orange 43, **43**
anti-war protests 30, 31, 32, 33, **33**, 34, 35, **35**, 36
ARVN (Army of the Republic of Vietnam) 16, 17, 18, **18**, 20, 24, 37, 38, 40, **41**, 42

Ball, George 31
Banks, Captain E. J. 26
Bao Dai 6, 13, 14
Bell UH-1 Huey **23**
boat people 44, **44**
bombing raids 20, **20**, 21, 37, 39
Buddhist protests 14, 18, **19**
Bui Tin 28
Burrows, Larry **30**

Calley, Lieutenant William 34
Cambodia 4, 8, 16, 36, **36**
casualty levels in Vietnam 31, 43, 44
Cedar Falls, Operation **27**
China 7, 9, 15, 20, 21, 44
communism 10, 11, **11**, 13, 29, 31, 33, 43, 44

Da Nang **21**, 42
defoliants 27, 43, **43**
de Gaulle, Charles 17
Diem see Ngo Dinh Diem
Dien Bien Phu, siege of 6, 7, **7**
domino theory, the 11, 31
draft, protests against the **33**
Dulles, John Foster 13

Easter Offensive 38, **38**
Eden, Anthony 7
Ehrhart, William 24
Eisenhower, Dwight D. 11, 12, 14
engagements, major 1965-7 **25**

Farley, James **30**
Ford, Gerald 41
France 4, 5, 13
French Indo-China 4, 5, **5**,

Geneva Conference 7, 8, **8**, 9, **9**, 10, 13
Giap see Vo Nguyen Giap
guerrilla warfare 6, 16, 24-5, 26, 29, 39
Gulf of Tonkin incident 18, 19
Gulf of Tonkin Resolution 19, 20

Hanoi 6, 21
Ho Chi Minh 4, **4**, 5, 6, 8, 13, **13**, 14, 15
Ho Chi Minh Trail 16, **25**
Hue 29, **29**, 42

Ia Drang Valley 23, 24
Iron Triangle **27**

Japan 5, 6, 10
Johnson, Lyndon B. 18, 19, 19, 20, 31

Kennedy, John F. 16, 17, **17**, 18, 19
Khe Sanh 28, **28**, 29
Kim Il-Sung 11
Kissinger, Henry 37, 39, **39**
Korean War, the 11-12, **12**

Laos 4, 8, 16, 37, **37**
Le Duc Tho 39, **39**
Linebacker, Operation 39
Lon Nol, General **36**

Maddox, USS 18
Magel, James **30**
Mao Zedong 6
McDonnell Douglas F4C **20**
McNamara, Robert 19, 32
military personnel in Vietnam, US 24, 27, 31, 36
My Lai massacre 33, 34, **34**

napalm 32, **32**
Navarre, General Henri 7
Ngo Dinh Diem 13, 14, **14**, 15, 16, 18
Nguyen Van Thieu 37, 42, 43
Nixon, Richard 33, 34, 35, 36, 37, 39, 40, 45
NLF (National Liberation Front) 16, 22,
North Vietnam 4, **8**, 13, **13**, 14, 16, 18, 20, 21, 39, 40, 41, 42, 43, 44
nuclear weapons 10
NVA (North Vietnamese Army) 15, 24, 28, 29, **32**, **37**, 42, **42**

Paris Peace Talks 39, **39**, 40
peace protests 34, 35, **35**, 36
Pentagon Papers, the 36

Phuoc Binh 41, 42
prisoners of war 40, **40**

Rather, Dan **31**
Reagan, Ronald **45**
Rolling Thunder, Operation 20, 21, 22

Saigon 6, **19**, 21, 29, 39, 42, **42**, 43
'search and destroy' tactics 22, 27
South Vietnam 4, **8**, 14, 16, 19, 20, 22, **25**, 29, 37, 38, 40, 41, 42, 43, 45
Soviet Union 7, 10, 11, 15, 20
Stevenson, Adlai 12
Strategic Hamlets policy **15**, 16, **16**
surrender of South Vietnam 43

television, influence of **31**, 32, 33
Tet Offensive, the 28, 29, 30, 32
Thich Quang Duc **19**
Thieu see Nguyen Van Thieu
Tho see Le Duc Tho
Tran Van, General 41

United States 4, 7, 10, 12, 13, 16, 18, 19, 22, 23, 30, 31, 34, 35, 36, 37, 38, 40, 41, 44
US military tactics 22-3
US personnel
  arrive in Vietnam 21, **21**
  inexperience of 26, 27
  missing in action (MIA) 44
  numbers in Vietnam 24, 27, 31, 36
  withdrawal from Vietnam 36, 43

Viet Cong 15, 16, 18, 20, 22, 24, 25, 26, 28, 29, **32**, 36, 38
Vietminh 4, **4**, 5, 6, **6**, 7, 8, 13, 14
Vietnam, division of 8, **8**, 9, 10, 13, 14
Vietnamization 37, **37**, 38
Vietnam Memorial **45**
Vietnam Veterans Against the War (VVAW) 34, **35**
Vo Nguyen Giap 4, 5, 6, 28, 29

Westmoreland, General William 22, **22**